TREETOPS

Stage 14
Teaching Notes

Jo Tregenza

Contents

Introduction	4
Comprehension strategies	6
Links to other TreeTops titles	7
Curriculum coverage chart	8

Five Children and It

Synopsis	11
Group or guided reading	12
Speaking, listening and drama activities	14
Writing activities	14

The Jungle Book

Synopsis	16
Group or guided reading	17
Speaking, listening and drama activities	19
Writing activities	19

The Secret Garden

Synopsis	21
Group or guided reading	22
Speaking, listening and drama activities	24
Writing activities	24

The Three Musketeers

Synopsis	26
Group or guided reading	27
Speaking, listening and drama activities	29
Writing activities	29

The Canterville Ghost

Synopsis	31
Group or guided reading	32
Speaking, listening and drama activities	34
Writing activities	34

White Fang

Synopsis	36
Group or guided reading	37
Speaking, listening and drama activities	39
Writing activities	39

Introduction

TreeTops Classics are abridged versions of classic texts especially chosen to appeal to 9- to 11-year-olds. They are ideal for use in group sessions and as model texts for writing. They are also an excellent stimulus for other writing activities and for speaking, listening and drama.

TreeTops Stages follow on from the Oxford Reading Tree Stages and are designed to be used flexibly, matched to individual pupils' reading ability.

How to introduce the books

Before reading the book, read the title and the blurb on the back cover. Ask the children what they think will happen. Read both authors' names (original author and abridger) and talk about books by the same authors that the children may have read or heard of. Look through the book briefly to find pictures of the main characters and discover the setting for the story.

Complete the reading session with the pupils telling you what they enjoyed about the story, encouraging them to refer to the text to support their reasons.

Using this Teaching Notes booklet

These Teaching Notes provide guidance for using the book with groups of pupils or with individuals. Suggestions are provided for group and guided reading, speaking, listening and drama, writing and cross-curricular links. The activities largely focus on strategies to increase comprehension (see the comprehension strategies grid on page 6) and include vocabulary development activities (a key part of improving comprehension).

In order to support your planning and record keeping, the curriculum coverage chart on pages 8–10 provides curriculum information relating to the curricula for England, Wales, Northern Ireland and Scotland. This includes PNS Literacy Framework objectives, Assessment Focuses and the reading, writing and speaking and listening levels children can reasonably be expected to be achieving when reading these TreeTops books.

Notes for adults and children in TreeTops Classics books

Included on the inside covers are notes to help parents/carers or classroom assistants share the books with children and questions to ask to help improve comprehension. (Answers to these are on the inside back cover of the books.) For children to read themselves there are:

- biographies of the original authors
- biographies of the abridging authors
- historical background information to help them understand the context of the story
- footnotes to explain difficult or archaic vocabulary.

Comprehension strategies

Book Title	Comprehension strategy taught through these Teaching Notes						
	Predicting	Questioning	Clarifying	Summarising	Imagining	Deducing
Five Children and It	✓	✓	✓	✓	✓	✓
The Jungle Book	✓	✓	✓	✓	✓	✓
The Secret Garden	✓	✓	✓	✓	✓	✓
The Three Musketeers	✓	✓	✓	✓	✓	✓
The Canterville Ghost	✓	✓	✓	✓	✓	✓
White Fang	✓	✓	✓	✓	✓	✓

Links to other treetops titles

TreeTops Classics Stage 14	Range	Other TreeTops Classics titles with similar ranges
Five Children and It	Classic fantasy story	Gulliver's Travels (Stage 15)
The Jungle Book	Classic animal story	Black Beauty (Stage 15) White Fang (Stage 14)
The Secret Garden	Classic realistic story	David Copperfield (Stage 15) Jane Eyre (Stage 16) Oliver Twist (Stage 16) Wuthering Heights (Stage 16)
The Three Musketeers	Classic adventure story	Moonfleet (Stage 15) Treasure Island (Stage 16) Robinson Crusoe (Stage 16) Kidnapped (Stage 16)
The Canterville Ghost	Classic ghost story	
White Fang	Classic animal story	The Jungle Book (Stage 14) Black Beauty (Stage 15)

Curriculum coverage chart

	Speaking, listening, drama	Reading	Writing
Five Children and It			
PNS Literacy Framework (Y5)	4.1	**V C**	9.2
National Curriculum (Y5)	Level 4	Level 4 AF 2, 3, 6	Level 4 AF 3
Scotland (5–14) (P6)	Level C, D	Level C, D	Level C, D
N. Ireland (P6/Y6)	Talking & Listening: 2, 7, 9, 11	3, 7, 1, 2, 4, 5, 6, 9, 12, 13	1, 2, 4, 6
Wales (Y5)	Range: 1, 5 Skills: 1, 6 Language & Development: 1	R: 1, 2, 3, 4, 5, 6 S: 1, 2, 3, 4, 5 L & D: 1, 2	R: 1, 2, 3, 4, 5 S: 1, 4 L & D: 4, 5, 6
The Jungle Book			
PNS Literacy Framework (Y5)	1.2	**V C** 7.2	9.5
National Curriculum (Y5)	Level 4	Level 4 AF 1, 2, 3	Level 4 AF 3
Scotland (5–14) (P6)	Level C, D	Level C, D	Level C, D
N. Ireland (P6/Y6)	Talking & Listening: 3, 4, 5, 11	1, 2, 3, 4, 5, 6, 7, 9, 12, 13	1, 2, 4, 5, 9
Wales (Y5)	Range: 1, 3, 4 Skills: 1, 2, 4, 5, 6, 7 Language & Development: 1, 4	R: 1, 2, 3, 4 S: 1, 2, 3, 4, 5 L & D: 1, 2	R: 1, 2, 3, 4, 5 S: 1, 3 L & D: 3, 4

C = Language comprehension   **V** = Vocabulary enrichment
AF = Assessment Focus   Y = Year   P = Primary

Curriculum coverage chart

	Speaking, listening, drama	Reading	Writing
The Secret Garden			
PNS Literacy Framework (Y5)	4.1	**V C** 8.2	9.3
National Curriculum (Y5)	Level 4	Level 4 AF 2, 3	Level 4 AF 1, 5
Scotland (5–14) (P6)	Level C, D	Level C, D	Level C, D
N. Ireland (P6/Y6)	Talking & Listening: 2, 3, 7, 8, 9	1, 2, 3, 4, 5, 6 7, 9, 10, 12, 13	1, 2, 3, 4,
Wales (Y5)	Range: 1, 4, 5, 6 Skills: 1, 5 Language & Development: 1, 2	R: 1, 2, 3, 5, 6 S: 1, 2, 3, 4, 5 L & D: 1, 2	R: 1, 2, 3, 4, 5 S: 1, 2, 4 L & D: 3, 4, 5, 6
The Three Musketeers			
PNS Literacy Framework (Y5)	4.2	**V C**	9.4
National Curriculum (Y5)	Level 4	Level 4 AF 2, 3, 6	Level 4 AF 1
Scotland (5–14) (P6)	Level C, D	Level C, D	Level C, D
N. Ireland (P6/Y6)	Talking & Listening: 2, 3, 5, 7, 9, 13	1, 2, 3, 4, 5, 6, 7, 9, 10, 11, 12, 13	1, 2, 4, 5, 6, 7, 10
Wales (Y5)	Range: 1, 2, 3, 4, 5, 6 Skills: 1, 2 Language & Development: 2, 4	R: 1, 2, 3, 5, 6 S: 1, 2, 3, 4, 5 L & D: 1, 2	R: 1, 2, 3, 4, 5 S: 1, 2, 3, 4 L & D: 1, 2

C = Language comprehension   **V** = Vocabulary enrichment
AF = Assessment Focus   Y = Year   P = Primary

Curriculum coverage chart

	Speaking, listening, drama	Reading	Writing
The Canterville Ghost			
PNS Literacy Framework (Y5)	1.1	**V** **C** 7.5	9.2
National Curriculum (Y5)	Level 4	Level 4 AF 3, 4, 5	Level 4 AF 7
Scotland (5–14) (P6)	Level C, D	Level C, D	Level C, D
N. Ireland (P6/Y6)	Talking & Listening: 2, 10, 11	1, 2, 3, 4, 5, 6, 7, 9, 10, 12, 13	1, 2, 3, 4, 5, 6, 7
Wales (Y5)	Range: 1, 2, 3 Skills: 1, 2, 3 Language & Development: 1, 2, 4	R: 1, 2, 3, 5, 6 S: 1, 2, 3, 4, 5 L & D: 1, 2	R: 1, 2, 3, 4, 5 S: 1, 2, 4 L & D: 2, 3, 4, 5, 6
White Fang			
PNS Literacy Framework (Y5)	1.3 4.1	**V** **C**	9.3
National Curriculum (Y5)	Level 4	Level 4 AF 2, 3	Level 4 AF 3
Scotland (5–14) (P6)	Level C, D	Level C, D	Level C, D
N. Ireland (P6/Y6)	Talking & Listening: 3, 4, 5, 7, 11	1, 2, 3, 4, 5, 6, 7, 9, 12, 13	1, 2, 3, 4, 5, 6
Wales (Y5)	Range: 1, 3, 5 Skills: 1, 2, 5, 6 Language & Development: 1	R: 1, 2, 3, 4, 5, 6 S: 1, 2, 3, 4, 5 L & D: 1, 2	R: 1, 2, 3, 4, 5 S: 1, 3, 4 L & D: 3, 4, 5, 6

C = Language comprehension   **V** = Vocabulary enrichment
AF = Assessment Focus   Y = Year   P = Primary

Five Children and It

Author: Edith Nesbit (1858–1924)

Synopsis: Five children move to a house in the countryside for the summer. The house is situated by an old chalk quarry and a gravel pit. Their father is called away on business and their mother must leave to look after their grandmother, who is ill. The children amuse themselves in the gravel pit and whilst digging they discover a buried 'Psammead' – an ancient sand fairy, who can grant wishes.

The children are allowed to make one wish a day but the results of their wishes cause mayhem and they are constantly in trouble with Martha, the housekeeper who looks after them.

Following some hair-raising adventures, the children manage to undo the problems caused by their wishes and they promise never to make a wish again.

Social and historical context:

The story is set in Edwardian England at the beginning of the twentieth century. The family's main home is in London, at the time when the environment is bleak and smog-ridden. The term 'pea-souper' became the classic phrase to describe London at this time and the smog gave rise to many respiratory illnesses.

The family is middle-class. The father is frequently away on business and a cook and housemaid help to run the house. The family are able to afford to spend long summer holidays in the countryside.

C = Language comprehension   **R, AF** = Reading Assessment Focus
V = Vocabulary enrichment   **W, AF** = Writing Assessment Focus

Group or guided reading

Introducing the book

C *(Clarifying, Deducing)* Read the title of the story. Ask the children: *What do you think 'It' is? Does it look friendly?*

C *(Predicting, Deducing)* Look at the picture of the house on the title page. Ask: *Can you guess when and where the book is set? Where do you think the house might be? Do you think it is a happy or a forbidding place? What makes you draw these conclusions?*

During reading

C *(Clarifying, Deducing)* Read up to the end of page 6 with the children, which includes the description of the garden and the surrounds of the house. Ask the children to draw what they imagine the scene looks like. Encourage them to think carefully about how they place things. For example, ask: *Where do you think the orchard might go?* Remind the children that visualising a scene helps the reader to understand and recall information and to engage with the story.

V Ask the children whether they know what a gravel pit is. If necessary, explain that it is a term that means an open pit used to extract gravel (round stones deposited in a river). Gravel pits normally lie in river valleys where the water table is high, so they fill naturally with water to form ponds or lakes.

Independent reading

- Ask the children to read the rest of Chapter 1 independently. Remind them to use a wide range of strategies to decode the text.

C *(Questioning, Deducing)* As they are reading ask the children to try to draw conclusions about the characteristics of each of the five children in the story. For example, ask: *Who is the dominant character? What do they all feel about 'the Lamb'?*

Assessment Check that children:

- *(R, AF2)* are able to describe the characters
- *(R, AF3)* can identify the relationships between the characters.
- Ask the children to finish reading to the end of the story independently.

Returning and responding to the text

C *(Summarising, Imagining)* When the children have read the whole story ask them to summarise the story so that someone else can understand it. Ask: *What did you think about the megatherium? Can you draw what it might look like?*

Assessment *(R, AF2)* Can the children summarise the story adequately?

C *(Clarifying, Deducing)* Discuss Chapter 2 'Beautiful as the day' with the children. Are they able to deduce the meaning behind this chapter? (The author is suggesting that vanity is a weakness and that the children should be happier with their true selves.)

C *(Clarifying)* Ask the children if they are able to identify the meaning behind the rest of the chapters. Why do they think that the Psammead always says that nothing good will come of their wishes?

Assessment *(R, AF6)* Have the children been able to recognise and understand the author's message behind the chapters?

Speaking, listening and drama activities

Objective Reflect on how working in role helps to explore complex issues (4.1).

- *(Imagining)* Go into role as the Psammead. What would children like to ask? What might they wish for? If children are confident, they might like to take the role of the Psammead.

Writing activities

Objective Experiment with different narrative forms and styles to write their own stories (9.2).

- *(Imagining)* Discuss the concept of wishes with the children. What would they wish for if they met the Psammead? Can they think about what might go wrong if their wish came true? What moral could be threaded into a chapter, if they wrote about the wish? For example, greed is never a good thing, selfishness might lose you friends, etc.

- Unpick one of the chapters in the story with the children. Can they identify the structure?

- Ask the children to write a new chapter for the story imagining a wish of their own. They should think carefully about how to structure the story and what moral will be illustrated.

Assessment *(W, AF3)* Can the children follow the structure within the story to write their own chapter?

Whole class reads

Sequels:
- *The Phoenix and the Carpet* and *The Story of the Amulet* by Edith Nesbit

Books on a similar theme:
- *Stig of the Dump* by Clive King

Cross-curricular links

Art
- Children could create models or pictures of the Psammead based on the description on pages 10–11.

History
- Look at pictures that show how people and society have changed over time. In particular, discuss the impact of the Industrial Revolution.

Geography
- Identify why and how places have changed, e.g. how gravel pits were formed.

I.C.T.
- Visit a virtual quarry at *www.virtualquarry.co.uk*

The Jungle Book

Author: Rudyard Kipling (1865–1936)

Synopsis: *The Jungle Book* creates a magical world in which animals can talk and reason. It tells the tale of a young human baby, Mowgli, found in the wilderness by a family of wolves and raised as one of their own. He makes many friends and several enemies along the way, but Mowgli's strongest relationships develop with Bagheera and Baloo. They help Mowgli to survive as he struggles with the threat of Shere Khan, the tiger. The story weaves a tale through the jungle as Mowgli grows and learns. Finally, he becomes restless and feels the pull of the man village.

Social and historical context: The original 1894 version of *The Jungle Book* was a collection of stories that Kipling had already published in magazines. Kipling had lived in India as a child and returned there as a journalist. At this time India was part of the vast British Empire and people in mainland Britain were keen to hear about the exotic far away places that formed part of the empire.

Kipling did a lot of travelling and in the nineteenth century this was the privilege of the wealthy. *The Jungle Book* evokes the different customs and ways of life in India in a way that is human and familiar, so that anybody can relate to the story no matter where they live.

C = Language comprehension   **R, AF** = Reading Assessment Focus
V = Vocabulary enrichment   **W, AF** = Writing Assessment Focus

Group or guided reading

Introducing the book

C *(Predicting)* Talk to the children about the title of the book. Children may have pre-conceived ideas about the book because of the cartoon film. Discuss what they know about the story. Can they name the main characters that they might discover?

C *(Deducing)* Ask: *What can you deduce about the image on the front cover? How might the bear and the panther be important to the story? Why does the boy have his arm round the bear?*

During reading

- Focus on the opening sentence. Why do the children think the author has chosen to open in this way?

V Read to the end of Chapter 1 with the children. Ask them to notice the vocabulary that has been used to describe the movement of the tiger, Mowgli and other animals, e.g. 'prowled', 'slunk' etc. Children could categorise the vocabulary into strong and weak movements.

C *(Imagining)* Act out some of the movement words to try to visualise the power of the movement of the different characters.

C *(Deducing)* Consider how the author has tried to use the vocabulary to describe movement as a way of hinting at the characteristics of the animals and to suggest a power relationship.

Assessment *(R, AF3)* Can the children read between the lines to explain the feelings behind an action?

Independent reading

- Ask the children to read to the end of Chapter 3.

- *(Deducing)* As they are reading ask them to try to build a clear picture of Mowgli's characteristics as he develops and grows.

Objective Infer writers' perspectives from what is written and from what is implied (7.2).

- *(Clarifying, Questioning)* Why do the children think that the author used a monkey as such a problematical character? Can children understand that the author is deliberately trying to challenge pre-conceived ideas?

Assessment Check that children:

- *(R, AF1)* can use the strategy of re-reading the text to gain different levels of meaning

- *(R, AF3)* can comment on the development of the characters.

- Ask the children to finish reading to the end of the story independently.

Returning and responding to the text

- *(Summarising)* When the children have read the whole story, ask them to summarise it to a friend who has not read the story.

- *(Clarifying, Deducing)* Ask: *What sort of character is Mowgli? What clues are there in the text to suggest this?* Explore the underlying message about prejudice with the children.

Assessment *(R, AF2)* Can the children understand and recall the main points and themes of the text?

Speaking, listening and drama activities

Objective Present a spoken argument, sequencing points logically, defending views with evidence and making use of persuasive language (1.2).

- Divide the children into two groups. Ask one group to prepare a spoken argument that persuades the wolf pack that Mowgli should be allowed to stay with them. The other half should argue against him staying. Encourage children to defend their points of view with evidence from the text.

Writing activities

Objective Create multi-layered texts, including use of hyperlinks and linked web pages (9.5).

- Discuss the use of instructional language and focus on the use of imperative verbs.

- Ask the children to think of their own jungle laws, such as, 'Never trust a monkey'. (Refer to Chapter 2.)

- Now ask them to think of why that statement is important, for example, 'Never trust a monkey because they are all liars.'

- Ask the children to devise and type their own jungle laws using connecting words to clarify why they must carry out that law.

- Once the statements have been created, ask the children to find a suitable picture, movie, sound clip or website on the internet that they can create a hyperlink to, for each law.

Assessment *(W, AF2)* Can the children make choices about presentation, appropriate to purpose and audience?

Whole class reads

Books on a similar theme:

- *Just So Stories* by Rudyard Kipling
- *Tarzan of the Apes* by Edgar Rice Burroughs
- *Jungle* (DK Eyewitness Book) by Theresa Greenway

Cross-curricular links

Art

- Use *Henri Rousseau's Jungle Book – Adventures in Art* by Doris Kutschbach to explore deceptively simple works of art on a jungle theme.

Geography

- Study a locality that is less economically developed.
- Recognise how people can improve damage to the environment, e.g. that has been caused by deforestation.

I.C.T.

- Compile a class book about the jungle by researching on the internet and using word processing or other software packages to present it.

The Secret Garden

Author: Frances Hodgson Burnett (1849–1924)

Synopsis: When her parents are killed by cholera, Mary Lennox is sent from India to live in England with her uncle. Misselthwaite Manor is a foreboding place with many rooms. In the gardens she meets the gardener Ben Weatherstaff and a robin. The robin becomes Mary's first friend. He helps her to find a key and a secret garden. As soon as she enters the garden, it becomes her own world.

One day she hears cries within the manor, and in a room behind a door she finds Colin Craven, her cousin. He cannot walk or stand and is so poorly that he never leaves his bedroom. Mary takes him in his wheelchair to visit the secret garden and here he begins his recovery.

Social and historical context: The story is set in late nineteenth and early twentieth century England, amongst the North Yorkshire Moors. At this time, India was still part of the British Empire. The story is set in a time when many families were extended and people often took in members of their wider family, such as cousins.

In the story Colin Craven makes himself better by thinking positively. The author was drawn to this belief after her eldest son died of tuberculosis.

C = Language comprehension **R, AF** = Reading Assessment Focus
V = Vocabulary enrichment **W, AF** = Writing Assessment Focus

Group or guided reading

Introducing the book

C *(Predicting)* Focus on the words in the title of the book. Ask the children: *Why might a garden be kept secret?*

V *(Clarifying)* Read the introductory passage on page 4 to the children. Do they know what cholera is? Explain that cholera is a disease caused by drinking contaminated water. Talk to the children about the British Empire.

During reading

C *(Deducing)* Read Chapter 1 with the children. Ask: *What can you deduce about Mary's relationship with her mother and father?*

C *(Questioning, Deducing)* Ask the children how they think Mary feels about her future. What comparisons do they think she makes between her former and new life? Encourage them to explain their answers using evidence from the text.

Assessment Check that children:

- *(R, AF3)* can comment on the development of the characters
- *(R, AF3)* can identify the relationships between the characters.

Independent reading

Objective Compare the usefulness of techniques such as visualisation, prediction and empathy in exploring the meaning of texts (8.2).

C *(Imagining)* Ask the children to read Chapter 2. Ask them to imagine that they are Mary and they have just been told about the secret garden.

C *(Imagining)* Invite the children to draw a picture of what they think the garden might look like. Then ask them to read Chapters 3–5. Encourage them to adapt their drawing based on what they are reading. Talk about how their images differ before and after reading more of the story. Are some things changed because of what is directly stated, whilst others have been altered because of what has been implied by the writer?

Assessment *(R, AF3)* Can children infer information beyond the literal from the text?

V Ask the children to collect vocabulary from the story that is unfamiliar to them or that they feel is particularly descriptive. Display the vocabulary and provide definitions where necessary.

● Ask the children to finish reading to the end of the story independently.

Returning and responding to the text

C *(Summarising)* When the children have read the whole story ask them to summarise the main themes, e.g. people (like plants) need care and attention in order to grow and develop.

Assessment *(R, AF2)* Can the children understand the themes underlying a whole text?

Speaking, listening and drama activities

Objective Reflect on how working in role helps to explore complex issues (4.1).

C *(Imagining, Deducing, Clarifying)* Challenge the children to create a freeze-frame image of the main characters in the secret garden at the moment that Mr Craven is about to enter. Encourage the children to think very carefully about their facial expressions. Ask them to explain how each person is feeling and why. Together, reflect on how the use of visual strategies such as freeze-frame images, have helped them to understand the story.

Writing activities

Objective Adapt non-narrative forms and styles to write fiction or factual texts, including poems (9.3).

- Re-read Chapter 4, which describes the garden. Ask the children to notice the vocabulary, language and style of the description. Focus particularly on the quality of vocabulary and the range of sentences.

- Provide a range of images of gardens or parks as a stimulus for writing. Discuss gardens that the children have seen.

- Invite the children to write a short description or a poem about a garden that inspires them.

Assessment *(W, AF1) Can the children write texts that are imaginative, interesting and thoughtful?*

- *(W, AF5) Can the children write short pieces that have varied sentence length and structure and use a wide range of connectives?*

Whole class reads
Books on a similar theme:
- *Tom's Midnight Garden* by Philipa Pearce
- *The Global Garden* by Kate Petty and Jennie Maizels
- *The Garden of Abdul Gasazi* by Chris Van Allsburg
- *The Paradise Garden* by Colin Thompson

Cross-curricular links
Art
- Create observational drawings of plants.

Science
- Discuss life processes common to plants.
- Make links between life processes in familiar plants and the environments in which they are found.

I.C.T.
- Take digital photographs of a garden to create a display. You could use images taken at different times of the year to create a stop-frame animation of a garden growing.

The Three Musketeers

Author: Alexandre Dumas (1802–1870)

Synopsis: 'All for one and one for all!' The three musketeers – Porthos, Aramis and Athos – are the most daring swordsmen in France and special bodyguards to the king. When d'Artagnan, a headstrong country boy, comes to Paris to join their ranks, they become the greatest friends of his life. When a villainous plot is hatched against the royal family by the sly cardinal, the four dashing blades must save them at any cost…

Social and historical context: Many of the characters who appear in The Three Musketeers were real people who are depicted reasonably accurately in the novel. King Louis XIII, his wife Queen Anne of Austria, and Cardinal Richelieu were important people during the period of the novel. Monsieur de Treville and Richelieu really were enemies and in 1642 de Treville was part of a plot to assassinate the cardinal. Richelieu did have his own personal company of guards, who shared a fierce rivalry with the musketeers. There was also tension between France and England at the time. The story is set in seveneenth century France, but was written by Dumas in the nighteenth century.

C = Language comprehension   **R, AF** = Reading Assessment Focus
V = Vocabulary enrichment   **W, AF** = Writing Assessment Focus

Group or guided reading

Introducing the book

(V) Ask the children if they know what musketeers are. (A musketeer was an infantry soldier in the 1600s equipped with a musket.)

During reading

(C) *(Deducing)* In Chapter 1 the author uses the word 'clopped' as d'Artagnan rides up to The Jolly Miller Inn. Ask the children: *Why do you think the author has used this particular word rather than 'galloped' or 'trotted'?*

(C) *(Imagining, Deducing)* Read Chapters 1 and 2. Try to help the children to picture the scene in Chapter 1 where the young and inexperienced d'Artagnan is attempting to fight with a much stronger and more experienced swordsman Ask: *What might the scene look like?* The children might like to act out this scene and consider some of the dialogue.

(C) *(Predicting)* Can the children predict who the man outside the inn might be? Is there any evidence in the text to support their views?

(C) *(Clarifying)* Ask the children: *What does the author write to suggest that this character will be important in the story?*

Assessment *(R, AF2)* Can the children refer to the text to support their views?

Independent reading

- Ask the children to work together to prepare a reading of Chapter 3. Encourage them to take on different roles. Remind them to read accurately and expressively.

Assessment *(R, AF1)* Can the children read expressively and fluently?

- Ask the children to finish reading to the end of the story independently.

Returning and responding to the text

C *(Summarising, Deducing)* When the children have read the whole story, ask them to talk about the different character traits of the three musketeers and d'Artagnan. Discuss how they all interact.

- Can the children think of modern comparisons with the three musketeers? Who might their 'superhero' be?

Assessment Check that children:

- *(R, AF2)* refer to the text to support their views
- *(R, AF3)* can identify the relationships between the characters.

C *(Questioning, Clarifying)* Ask the children to work in collaborative groups to generate any questions that they have. Are there any points that are not clear or they don't understand?

Objective Infer writers' perspectives from what is written and from what is implied (7.2).

C *(Questioning, Deducing)* Talk to the children about the viewpoint of the author. This story is clearly in favour of the French king and queen, and the musketeers. Discuss how the story might be different if it were written with sympathy for the cardinal.

C *(R, AF6)* Can the children identify the author's viewpoint?

Speaking, listening and drama activities

Objective Perform a scripted scene making use of dramatic conventions (4.2).

- Discuss how the children will recreate a key scene from the story to perform, asking them to agree on which scene they will use.

- Briefly revise the dramatic conventions that are used in a play. Give them time to decide what the characters will say, how they will say it, what gestures and body language they will use and how tension will be built up.

- Allow them time to practise and ask the children to appraise each other's performances. Were there any lines they would say or do differently?

Writing activities

Objective Develop viewpoint through the use of direct speech, portrayal of action and selection of detail (9.4).

- Discuss which chapter in the book could be re-written as a playscript. Draw the children's attention to chapters with plenty of dialogue and a reasonable number of characters.

- Demonstrate how to set out text for a playscript.

- Remind children of dramatic conventions such as sound effects, stage directions, etc.

- Ask them to re-write their chosen chapter as a playscript.

Assessment *(W, AF1)* Can the children write imaginative playscripts that maintain characterisation and use a range of stylistic features for effect?

Whole class reads

Books on a similar theme:

- *France: Horrible Histories* by Terry Deary
- *A Tale of Two Cities* by Charles Dickens

Cross-curricular links

Art
- Look at French Renaissance art.

Geography/Modern Foreign Languages
- Learn about France and French culture.

History
- Research French society in the 1600s, focusing on what types of clothing people wore.

The Canterville Ghost

Author: Oscar Wilde (1854–1900)

Synopsis: The Otis family move from America to live in an old haunted house in England – Canterville Chase. The resident ghost, Sir Simon de Canterville, killed his wife in 1575 and his guilt causes him to haunt the house where it happened. Sir Simon haunts with different coloured bloodstains that appear on the floor every day. It is all to no avail as nothing frightens the Otis family, especially the naughty twins! Virginia Otis, the only girl, feels sorry for Sir Simon and when he tells her that his wife's death was an accident and how unhappy and lonely he is, she tries to help him.

Social and historical context: The book is set in the late nineteenth century, a period marked by the rise of a growing middle class in Great Britain. This middle class had gained wealth through the technological advances of the Industrial Revolution, and as a result of Britain's expanding empire. The values of this class stood in marked contrast to the values of an older aristocracy – which the ghost comes from. The middle class idealised the importance of the family, thrift and hard work, and this book shows a clash not just between the aristocracy and the middle classes, but also between British and American cultures.

C = Language comprehension **R, AF** = Reading Assessment Focus
V = Vocabulary enrichment **W, AF** = Writing Assessment Focus

Group or guided reading

Introducing the book

C *(Predicting)* Look at the title and the cover. What genre do the children think the story will be based on? Activate children's prior understanding by asking whether they know of any other ghost stories. Ask: *What usually happens in ghost stories?*

During reading

C *(Clarifying, Predicting)* Read Chapter 1 together. Ask: *Why do you think the family might have moved to England from America? What do you notice about the names of the two older children in the book? How do these names give us a clue about the nature of the family?*

C *(Deducing)* Ask: *What can you deduce about the Otis family having read Chapter 1? What evidence can you find in the text to support your view?*

Objective Explore how writers use language for comic and dramatic effects (7.5).

V Ask: *How has the author used the dialogue for Mrs Umney to suggest her characteristics?* Challenge the children to be word detectives and collect examples of words that can suggest someone has an accent.

Assessment *(R, AF5)* Can the children begin to explain the literary devices that the author has used to suggest characteristics?

C *(Imagining)* Ask the children to draw a picture or use a small world model to re-create the scene as the family first arrive at the house.

(C) *(Clarifying)* As they read, ask the children to notice how the author switches from one scene (the Otis family) to another (watching Simon de Canterville). Ask: *What effect does this have on the reader in terms of how you feel about the ghost?*

(C) *(Questioning)* Ask the children to work in pairs to develop questions to ask Sir Simon.

- When the children have finished reading, go into role as Sir Simon and answer the children's questions.

Assessment Check that children:

- *(R, AF3)* are able to make connections between different moments in the text

- *(R, AF4)* can identify structure and understand how the scenes switch and focus on different characters.

- Ask the children to finish reading to the end of the story independently.

Returning and responding to the text

(C) *(Summarising, Clarifying)* When the children have read the whole book, ask them to retell the story. Then ask them to consider how the author has chosen to vary the presentation of the story.

(C) *(Questioning)* Are the children surprised by how the story turns out, because this ghost story is more a humorous tale than a spooky ghost story?

Assessment *(R, AF5)* Can the children identify the different devices that the author has used?

Speaking, listening and drama activities

Objective Tell a story using notes designed to cue techniques, such as repetition, recap and humour (1.1).

- Ask the children to recall any ghost stories that they know. Invite them to retell their ghost story to the class. Encourage them to prepare by using notes and cue techniques such as repetition, rather than reading directly from a written text.

Writing activities

Objective Experiment with different narrative form and styles to write their own stories (9.2).

- Discuss familiar ghost stories with the children.
- Define the common features of a ghost story.
- Revisit the pages in the text where Mrs Umney gives warnings in rhyme, e.g. 'A flock of crows, a bleak storm blows'.
- Highlight vocabulary that is adventurous.
- Challenge the children to write their own ghost stories that must include a warning rhyme modelled on how Mrs Umney speaks in the text.

Assessment *(W, AF7)* Can the children demonstrate the sustained use of varied, precise and often adventurous vocabulary?

Whole class reads
Books on a similar theme:
- *The Ghost of Thomas Kempe* by Penelope Lively
- *The Orchard Book of Goblins, Ghouls and Ghosts and Other Magical Stories* by Martin Waddell and Tony Ross
- *The Great Ghost Rescue* by Eva Ibotson

Cross-curricular links
History
- Research Britain and the wider world in Tudor times, which is the period in which Sir Simon and his wife were alive, and then research Victorian times, when the Otises inhabited Canterville Chase.

Design & Technology
- Create one of the rooms that is central to the story, either in a doll's house or in a shoe box. For example, the room with the fireplace where the bloodstains appear, or the room that Sir Simon hides in.

Art
- Research William Morris, the Victorian artist and designer, and his work.

I.C.T.
- Use a computer package to design a repeating pattern to make Victorian-style wallpaper (similar to William Morris designs).

Science
- Create circuits to make a light for the recreated room.

White Fang

Author: Jack London (1876–1916)

Synopsis: *White Fang* tells the story of how a wolf is gradually transformed into a dog. He is half-dog, half-wolf and the only survivor in his litter. The story is told mainly from his point of view. He starts life in the wild with his mother Kiche, but then they are kept and trained by Grey Beaver, a Native American. Grey Beaver is a kind but firm owner but White Fang clashes with Lip-Lip, a working dog also kept by the tribe. White Fang is taken to Fort Yukon on a trip to trade furs, where Grey Beaver is tricked into selling him. White Fang is beaten and turned into a fighting dog, but two men save him and treat him with kindness. In time he responds and is tamed.

Social and historical context: *White Fang* is set in the Yukon region of North America where western Canada borders Alaska. This region was controlled by The Hudson's Bay Company until it was purchased in 1870 by the Canadian government. In the 1890s this area's population rapidly increased because of 'gold fever' during the Klondike Gold Rush.

This was a time of trading posts, fur trappers, Native Americans, miners, gold prospectors and the origins of the Canadian Mounted Police. The story explores civilisation and nature, and the violence and morality that exists in both these spheres. Ultimately it is a tale of redemption as the wild wolf-dog responds to kind owners.

C = Language comprehension   **R, AF** = Reading Assessment Focus
V = Vocabulary enrichment   **W, AF** = Writing Assessment Focus

Group or guided reading

Introducing the book

(C) *(Predicting)* Focus on the front cover. Ask the children: *What conclusions can you draw about the characteristics of the wolf? Do his eyes give any clues?*

(V) *(Clarifying)* Look at a map of North America and find the Yukon region. Discuss the features of its landscape with the children. Ensure they become familiar with some of the vocabulary related to the setting. Children might like to look into the background of Native Americans to support their understanding.

During reading

(C) *(Clarifying, Summarising)* Read the first two chapters together, taking opportunities for individual children to read sections to the others. Once the reading is finished ask the children to summarise what they have understood so far.

(C) *(Clarifying)* Can the children identify the two main characters in the book? What do they understand has happened so far? Take the opportunity to clarify any misunderstandings.

(C) *(Questioning, Deducing)* How do the children feel about the way the author describes the death of the four cubs in such a matter-of-fact way? Why do they think the author has handled it in this way? This question will introduce children to the themes of natural selection and nature's hierachy of predators.

Assessment Check that children:

- *(R, AF2)* can understand, retrieve and summarise information from the text
- *(R, AF3)* can deduce why the author has described the events in the way he has.

White Fang

C *(Predicting)* Now read Chapter 3 together. Discuss with the children how this chapter sets up the strong relationship between the mother and the cub. Can the children predict what might happen between the two animals?

Independent reading

C *(Imagining, Summarising)* The children should read Chapters 4–7 independently. Tell the children that when they have finished reading you are going to ask them to create three freeze-frame images that will summarise and explain the plot so far.

Assessment *(R, AF2)* Can the children choose key scenes that demonstrate the mains points of the text?

- Ask the children to finish reading to the end of the story independently.

Returning and responding to the text

C *(Clarifying)* When the children have read the whole story, ask them to talk about how they felt as they read the story. Did it evoke an emotional response from the readers? If so, how did the author achieve this?

Assessment *(R, AF6)* Can the children comment on the overall effect of the text on the reader?

Speaking, listening and drama activities

Objective Use and explore different question types (1.3). Reflect on how working in role helps to explore complex issues (4.1).

C *(Questioning, Imagining)* Ask the children to work in pairs to develop questions that they would like to ask White Fang, Grey Beaver, Kiche and Scott. Some children could go into role as these characters so that they can have the opportunity to gain some answers to the questions.

Writing activities

Objective Adapt non-narrative forms and styles to write fiction or factual texts (9.3).

- Discuss the characteristics of White Fang.

- Identify examples in the text where figurative writing has been used to describe characteristics.

- Demonstrate how to write a character profile by modelling a profile of Kiche.

- Provide a planning structure to support children's writing, e.g. introduction with background information, physical appearance, main character trait, secondary trait, hopes and desires.

- Provide interesting paper, e.g. paper with a wolf outline, for children to write their character profile.

Assessment *(W, AF3)* Can the children use clues from the text, both literal and implied, to create a character profile of White Fang that has a clear structure?

Whole class reads

Companion novel:

- *Call of the Wild* by Jack London. (A tale of a domestic dog that reverts to living as a wild animal.)

Books on a similar theme:

- *The Wolves of Willoughby Chase* by Joan Aitken
- *Wolves in the Wall* by Neil Gaiman
- *Eye of the Wolf* by Daniel Pennac

Cross-curricular links

Geography

- Make maps of the Yukon and plot the journey of White Fang. Use atlases, globes, maps and plans to gain experience in using secondary sources of information, including aerial photographs.

I.C.T.

- Use an internet search programme such as 'Google Earth' to identify the landscape of the book.

History

- Research the Klondike Gold Rush.
- Research the origins of the Canadian Mounted Police.